# RUGGIE RULES

## for choosing and working with a financial advisor

Thomas H. Ruggie, ChFC®, CFP®

with

Louis Shinaman, ChFC®
and
Jorge A. Romero, CFP®

Ruggie Rules

Published by:
90-Minute Books
302 Martinique Drive
Winter Haven, FL 33884
www.90minutebooks.com

Published in the United States of America

ISBN-13: 978-0692535165
ISBN-10: 0692535160

For more information on 90-Minute Books including finding out how you can publish your own lead generating book, visit www.90minutebooks.com or call (863) 318-0464

Here's what's inside…

# RUGGIE RULES

# Introduction

**Taking root...**

Did you know that the fastest-growing metropolitan area in the United States in 2014 and 2015 was not an oil town like Houston or Dallas, nor was it a coastal resort town like Myrtle Beach?

It was a Central Florida Baby-Boomer boomtown called The Villages®, a community which more than doubled its population from 51,442 residents in 2010 to a number that soared above 114,000 in 2014.

In The Villages® community, "active seniors" focus on living their lives, not just observing the years go by. With nearly 45 golf courses, 2,500 clubs and activities, abundant restaurants, shopping, entertainment, and world-class healthcare, this community holds a special charm for many interested in spending their golden years in the glow of the sun.

Not only is the community growing, so is its job base, which has expanded by 186% since 2001, according to *Forbes Magazine*. In addition, personal income growth, largely from assets owned by seniors, has soared by some 60% since 2000, which is 10 times the national average growth rate of 6%.

In other words, this is a prime location for financial advisors who counsel retirees.

Why, then, was I was so reluctant to take our nationally recognized wealth management process – refined over 25 years of helping hundreds of clients preparing for, nearing, or living out their retirement years – a mere 35 minutes down the road to serve residents of The Villages® community? What powerful force was holding me back from opening an office of Ruggie Wealth Management there?

Once I understood the answer to that question, not only was I able to open an office in the heart of that growth area, but I was able to see the rules I live by professionally take root.

## So what did I learn?

For more than 10 years I had watched the actions, protocols, and sales tactics of many financial advisors who counsel retirees in Florida. While a core group of quality advisors exists here, I believe those good advisors get overshadowed by individuals who peddle products that line their own pockets, and do so with little or no regard for the needs of their clients.

It would not be too much of a stretch to say that most Florida retirees in communities could enjoy a free lunch – AND free breakfast and dinner, too – almost every day of the week, courtesy of product peddlers, many of whom call themselves "financial advisors." And, as we know, there just simply are no free lunches.

In fact, according to a report by the U.S. Securities and Exchange Commission (SEC), North American Securities Administrators Association (NASAA), and Financial Industry Regulatory Authority (FINRA), called *Protecting Senior Investors: Report of Examinations of Securities Firms Providing "Free Lunch" Sales Seminars* (Sept. 2007), between April

2006 and June 2007 the Securities and Exchange Commission audited over 110 firms in high-retiree-concentration states such as Florida, Texas, Tennessee, California, and North Carolina. Overwhelmingly the SEC found that many sales seminars advertised as "educational," "learning workshops," and/or stating "nothing will be sold at this workshop" were actually simple fronts for sales pitches even when advertisements did not mention any specific investment products.

Perhaps I was getting in my own way. I simply did not want to establish an office in The Villages® community just to see the reputation I'd worked nearly 25 years to build get tarnished by the perception that we, too, were in the same product-peddling business.


## What changed?

A little more than a year ago, we consulted a marketing company in California that helps financial advisory firms across the country and asked them to help us fine-tune our message about the financial planning process we walk clients through. Having just hired a new financial advisor, our goal was to put together some marketing materials for the unique, four-step planning process we call Ruggie WealthCare℠.

The marketing company was very excited about our process and the impact it was having on the financial well-being of retirees. They asked how much of our current and potential client base consisted of retirees. They were shocked to learn of our proximity to The Villages® community. What shocked them even more was that, armed with what they called a "fantastic retirement planning process," we had purposely avoided having a presence in the huge market that was right in our own backyard.

It was at that moment we made the decision to open an office that would serve people from within The Villages® community. We went in committed to providing the financial integrity, benefit, and value the thousands of retirees living in – and moving to – this area deserved. Instead of worrying about being painted with the same broad strokes as the product-peddlers, we set out to paint a whole new picture of what financial investing and advising should be.

## What are the Ruggie Rules?

The Ruggie Rules are the rules I live by professionally and insist my team live by as well. They are not just part of our firm's culture. They are part of our lives.

Whether you use our services or not, we want you to be able to benefit from the Ruggie Rules. Use them as a basis of comparison before you select an advisor. If you're considering making a change from your current advisor, use them to develop a checklist or to frame the questions you want answered. I won't deny that these rules place the way we do business in a good light. Once you understand what's behind them, we think you will agree that they make companies that adhere to them the types of firms you WANT to do business with.

Ruggie Rules advocate on behalf of investors. In the case of those nearing or entering retirement, they don't just address growing and preserving your wealth, they look at growing and preserving your quality of life and peace-of-mind throughout your golden years.

To Your Continued Success!

*Thomas Ruggie*

# RUGGIE RULES

# I. Be intentional in picking your advisor

### RULE 1. IF IT SEEMS TOO GOOD TO BE TRUE, IT PROBABLY IS.

Hindsight is crystal clear. There were many painful lessons to be learned from financial frauds such as the one perpetrated by Bernie Madoff on his unsuspecting investors.

These are just a few indicators that should have raised red flags for investors:

- He was unwilling to describe his investment strategy.

- He only "invited" specific investors to join his "investing" group, and those who questioned his strategy would find themselves uninvited.

- He issued "customer statements."

- He reported positive returns in all market environments.

These are some of the takeaways:

- Your advisor should be willing to explain his or her plan for your money, including any proprietary processes, until you have no more questions left. You should fully understand your financial plan, including how your investments are being allocated and why. Every aspect of your relationship with your advisor should be transparent.

- Your advisor should be running a business, not a club. If you feel like you're being singled out and given a unique opportunity to invest that others are not, ask why.

When advisors claim extraordinary skills and results, check with respected third parties, such as Morningstar.

- You should receive your financial statements from an independent, third-party custodian. You need to know that the value of your securities reported by a third-party custodian is equal to the value of your securities reported by your advisor.

- There are risks to investing. If someone tells you that they guarantee results that perform as well as the market with less risk, run away.

## RULE 2. DON'T WORK WITH AN 'ADVISOR' WHO ONLY SELLS ANNUITIES OR SINGLE PRODUCTS.

Some 'advisors' only have the ability to sell annuities. These individuals also tend to be the best salespeople. Not surprisingly, they will always push annuities and never evaluate what else may be best for you as the client.

The key is not to utilize an advisor ONLY licensed to sell insurance products or other single products. As you've probably guessed by now, I'm not a big fan of annuities for many reasons. In fact, I've created a whole section about annuities later in the book to expound on this subject.

First of all, annuities are not bought, they're SOLD to you, often without your full understanding of them. You will likely receive biased information, and you will not be provided with all of the options necessary to consider when planning for a healthy retirement. Annuities and similar products can tie your money up for prolonged periods of time, keeping you from taking advantage of better investment opportunities for your financial future.

Consider this true account: An 83-year-old man was sold an annuity that put his life savings into a 30-year annuity with a 15-year surrender clause. This meant he couldn't touch the majority of his money until he turned 98 unless he wanted to pay a penalty, a problem his children had to live with when it became necessary to use their dad's limited funds for his nursing care. As he became increasingly debilitated, they drained their own savings to keep from decimating their dad's investment with penalties.

### RULE 3. EXPERIENCE COUNTS.

It matters whether an advisor has spent many years in the business. Part of the value an advisor brings to his or her clients is the perspective gained from working with other clients. You don't want your advisor using your money to learn on the job.

### RULE 4. INSIST ON A REGISTERED INVESTMENT ADVISOR WHO WORKS IN YOUR BEST INTEREST.

Currently, just about anyone can legally call himself or herself a "financial planner" or "financial advisor," even those with little knowledge and no licensure. This is especially true of the army of annuity salespeople, who often use these terms to give themselves a level of credibility they haven't earned.

A minimal standard, called "the suitability standard," states that as long as an investment is reasonably suited for the client, the advisor is free to use it as long as it is reasonably suited for that transaction.

We believe that standard is too low.

Who can you trust? Start by narrowing the vast field to independent Registered Investment Advisors (RIAs) & fee-only financial planners who are voluntarily held to higher standards of care. As fiduciaries, these advisors must legally and ethically put their clients' best interests ahead of their own.

RIAs are legally answerable to state or federal authorities. Authorities are empowered to conduct spot audits and require a relatively high standard of compliance.

All Registered Investment Advisory firms must give prospective clients copies of their compliance paperwork (called Form ADV) filed with regulators. What's in these detailed reports? They include details about fees, educational background, work experience, and investment/planning methodology.

If you enter a Registered Investment Advisory firm or advisor name into this website, http://www.sec.gov/investor/brokers.htm, you can access the Form ADV (compliance paperwork) and see if there is any record of violations or misconduct.

## RULE 5. KNOW WHICH DESIGNATIONS ARE PREFERRED, WHICH ONES ARE LEGITIMATE, AND WHICH ONES YOUR ADVISOR HAS EARNED.

Your financial team should have invested the time and education necessary to earn professional certification by the industry's trusted certification and accreditation bodies.

Having a designation or multiple designations does not necessarily make one advisor better than another. It does show, to some degree, how seriously an advisor takes his or her profession. How much more is the advisor willing to work to develop more knowledge and a better education? Top-Tier designations available to financial advisors include: CFA® (Chartered Financial Analyst), CFP® (Certified Financial Planner™ Professional), and ChFC® (Chartered Financial Consultant).

| CFA | CFP | ChFC |
|---|---|---|
| Undergraduate degree or combination of college and full-time work experience adding up to four years | Bachelor's degree (or higher) from an accredited college or university and three years of full-time personal financial planning experience or equivalent part-time experience (2,000 hours equals 1 year full-time) | Three years of full-time business experience within the five years preceding the awarding of the designation |
| 250 hours of study for each of the 3 levels Three six-hour course exams | Completion of a CFP-board-registered program or possession of one of the following: CPA ChFC Chartered Life Underwriter (CLU) | Seven core and 2 elective courses, equivalent of 27 semester credit hours Proctored exam for each course |

| | | |
|---|---|---|
| | CFA | |
| | Ph.D. in business or economics | |
| | Doctorate of Business Administration | |
| | Attorney's License | |
| | Final certification exam | |

Unfortunately, some designations can be earned with minimal or no study. Some advisors use less rigorous or dubious designations to win the trust of older and/or wealthier clients.

For example, a respected CFA® designation requires roughly 900 hours of study and three 6-hour course exams, where a CFRA (Certified Retirement Financial Advisor) is a much less rigorous designation, requiring students to invest 40 to 75 hours of preparation and to pass one 100-question test.

| CFA: Chartered Financial Analyst | CFRA: Certified Retirement Financial Advisor |
| --- | --- |
| Approx. 900 hours of study | Approx. 40-75 hours of study |
| Accounting, economics, ethics, finance, math | One 100-question exam |
| Three 6-hour exams | |

You can learn more by visiting www.finra.org/investors/professional-designations. This site will help you decode the letters that sometimes follow a financial professional's name. You can also see whether the issuing organization requires continuing education, takes complaints, and has a way for you to confirm who holds the credential. FINRA also indicates which of the credentials it monitors, although it doesn't endorse any professional credential or designation.

## RULE 6. DO A PROPER BACKGROUND CHECK ON YOUR FINANCIAL ADVISOR.

Make sure there is no past litigation surrounding him or her. If there is, determine if this is grounds for looking elsewhere.

By far, the easiest way to check up on your advisor is to visit FINRA's BrokerCheck (http://brokercheck.finra.org/Search/Search); there you can learn about your advisor's past employment history, licenses, and other qualifications. BrokerCheck is a database of formerly and currently licensed financial professionals. The database is maintained by the Financial Industry Regulatory Authority, a self-regulatory organization that oversees most, but not all, financial advisors.

**Note: Insurance-only licensed persons won't generally be found here, as they don't meet the requirements for inclusion in these databases because they don't hold securities licenses.**

## *RULE 7. LOOK AT RESPECTED PROFESSIONAL RECOGNITION AS ONE MORE BENCHMARK.*

Is the advisory team well-respected among their peers? Do industry leaders seek their insights or thought leadership?

In and of itself, recognition from leaders and respected organizations in the field does not necessarily make one financial advisory firm better than another, but we believe the hard work required of advisors to earn national attention from those leaders in our field lends credibility to the way they do business.

### *RULE 8. ENGAGE A FINANCIAL TEAM.*

You want a team backing you up, whether in sports, business, or your personal finances. Members of your financial team should help ensure each investment decision is made within the context of your overall financial strategy.

Members of your financial team may consist of a senior financial advisor, associate financial advisor, portfolio manager, client relationship manager, primary client service manager, etc. They should keep up with you and your progress through a series of ongoing steps.

They should be able to work comfortably with your attorneys, tax advisors, and other professionals. Through strategic alliances, they should be able to help you coordinate your financial plan with:

- o 401(k) plans/retirement plans
- o Legal/estate planning
- o Business planning (succession planning, employee benefits, tax planning, etc.)
- o Insurance review/planning
- o Tax planning
- o Mortgages (new and refinancing)
- o Marketing
- o Property/casualty insurances

A strong team can deliver a better experience to you, something even the best-intentioned individual will find it hard to do all on his or her own.

## RULE 9. YOUR FINANCIAL FIRM SHOULD GET THE LITTLE THINGS RIGHT.

Once a financial advisor ensures the big things are done to, at the very least, a satisfactory level (such as investment performance, proactive contact, and overall client management), it is often the little things that distinguish a good advisor from a great one. I've always looked at this like a jigsaw puzzle: The more little pieces that can be added to the puzzle for clients, the clearer the overall picture is going to be. I've found that "little things," like promptly returning phone calls or emails, immediately taking action when a need arises, making timely phone calls when a client has had an adverse situation, proactively reaching out with well wishes for special occasions such as birthdays, and just checking in to see how things are going, are not "little" at all.

# II. Most retirees benefit from professional financial assistance

### RULE 10. YOU AND YOUR FAMILY SHOULD HAVE YOUR OWN "CFO."

It's a good idea to engage a financial advisor when…

- o You want your finances to be well-managed but don't know where to start.
- o You don't have the time or sufficient expertise to do your own financial planning.
- o You have an immediate need or life event that could change your financial picture.
- o You prefer having a plan and clear goals you can track to make certain you stay on target.

### RULE 11. ONLY 15% OF INVESTORS SHOULD HANDLE THEIR OWN INVESTMENTS.

It is my belief, based on about 25 years of experience, that approximately 15% of the investor population can or should realistically handle their own investments, while the other 85%, the so-called "uninvolved investors," should not attempt to manage their own investments - at least not without professional oversight. To do so takes lots of time, dedication, knowledge, and, most importantly, the ability to handle the emotional highs and lows that can occur during various market cycles.

Statistics show that most people who handle their own investments have a tendency to buy and sell at the wrong times, buying more during euphoric times and selling more during crises. Remember the tech bubble of the late 1990s and the 2008 financial crisis? It should not come as a surprise, yet it is very alarming, that the majority of the money invested during these bubbles is invested in the later stages, after solid returns have already been made. Common sense tells us that investors shouldn't panic or try to time the market, yet the majority of investors underperform compared to market indexes because they do just that, letting their emotions cloud their judgment.

Working with a trusted advisor who has a written strategy and processes in place can keep you from falling prey to investment performance killers such as greed and fear.

Even when someone is part of the 15% that can handle investing themselves, often their spouses are not. This can create some problems should the involved investor pre-decease his or her spouse. During my career, I've experienced at least a dozen situations where I've met with a couple that had been doing their own investing and doing fairly well. They come to me to develop a relationship in order to create a succession plan for managing their assets and investments in case the more involved spouse pre-deceases the less or uninvolved spouse.

It is not uncommon among retired couples that the husband is the primary decision-maker for financial affairs, yet, statistically, the wife often outlives him. Therefore, it's important that both spouses have some level of involvement in their collective financial plan and a trusted relationship to fall back on.

**Note: For years I've been a big fan of John Bogle, the finance pioneer who founded The Vanguard Group. I've read John's books and certainly agree with the majority of his views; however, I've always struggled with Vanguard's push away from the use of financial advisors toward a do-it-yourself model.**

In fact, it was not until recently that Vanguard changed direction in terms of their thoughts on the use of an advisor and completed numerous studies to show the long-term benefit investors have with the use of qualified financial advisors.

Recent Vanguard research by Francis M. Kinniry Jr., Colleen M. Jaconetti, Michael A. DiJoseph, and Yan Zilbering shows that "...advisors not only add peace of mind, but also may add about three percentage points of value in net portfolio returns over time." They state, "Your advisor has the ability and the time to evaluate your portfolio investments, meet with you to discuss objectives, and help get you through tough markets.

They also add, "Your advisor can work with you to create a diversified portfolio, while ensuring you don't pay too much for investments or in taxes on investment returns. Wealth management entails making regular changes to your portfolio to help reduce risk, and when you're ready to withdraw, you can do it in such a way to help limit the taxes you pay."

A balanced, diversified investor has fared relatively well

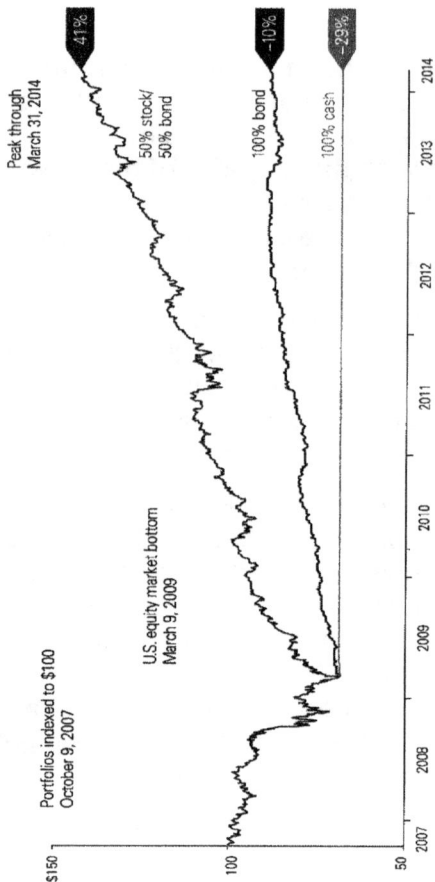

$150

Portfolios indexed to $100
October 9, 2007

Peak through
March 31, 2014

41%

50% stock/
50% bond

U.S. equity market bottom
March 9, 2009

100

-10%

100% bond

-29%

100% cash

50

2007    2008    2009    2010    2011    2012    2013    2014

Source: FactSet.

Notes: The 50% stock/50% bond portfolio is represented by the Standard & Poor's 500 Index and the Barclays U.S. Aggregate Bond Index (rebalanced monthly). The 100% bond portfolio is represented by the Barclays U.S. Aggregate Bond Index. The 100% cash portfolio is represented by 3-month Treasury bills.

*Past performance is no guarantee of future results. The performance of an index is not an exact representation of any particular investment, as you cannot invest directly in an index.*

This is a hypothetical illustration.

**Your Financial Advisor Can Provide:**

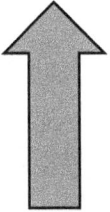

Guidance
Diversification
Potentially higher net returns
Behavioral coaching

Potentially less cost
Potentially less risk

# III. You must have a well-thought-out, strategic plan

I believe that while many can't express it, deep down, most retirees are looking for clarity and simplicity in their lives. Financially, this is something we strongly feel is attained through the development and implementation of a well-thought-out and executed financial plan and investment strategy, which also includes careful monitoring after implementation and proactive adjustments when needed.

### RULE 12. DON'T ACCEPT A COOKIE-CUTTER FINANCIAL PLAN.

Find a firm willing to evaluate your entire situation, ask the proper questions, and develop a customized plan for your needs and goals.

### RULE 13. DON'T MISTAKE A FINANCIAL PLAN'S FORM FOR SUBSTANCE.

Many big banks and wirehouses, with their huge marketing budgets, are notorious for producing glitzy, glossy reports, often with dozens of pages of charts and pictures. In reality, these are often "paint-by-number" programs that rely on limited data inputs to spit out "custom" reports.

These beautifully produced reports often help paint the picture that these firms are in the business of financial planning. Yet, often, any real customized planning is limited or reserved for their highest-net-worth clientele. Most clients receive what they say are financial plans but are actually proprietary investment plans in disguise. Once this type of plan is put in place, the firm creating it will often set it and forget it.

## RULE 14. GOOD FINANCIAL PLANS TRANSCEND THE NOISE OF THE MARKETS.

A good financial plan looks well beyond the hot trends to really focus on you and your family's needs across time. Your advisor should remain continuously engaged with you, returning to the plan and making adjustments to ensure you stay on track as much as possible when achieving your financial goals.

Figure 15. The importance of maintaining discipline: Reacting to market volatility can jeopardize return

What if the "drifting" investor fled from stocks after the 2008 plunge?

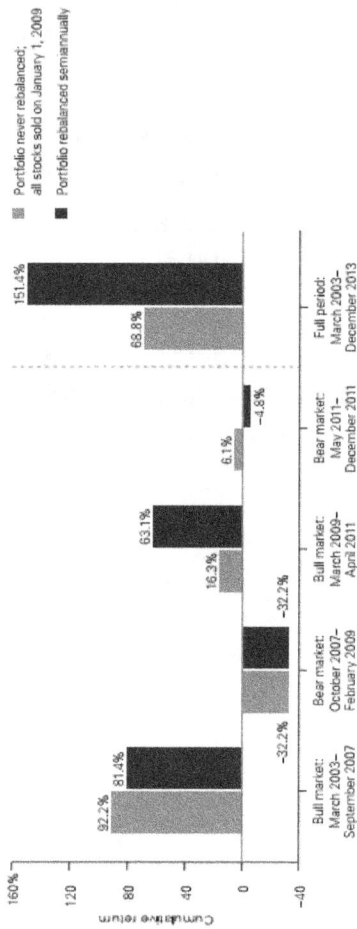

Legend:
- Portfolio never rebalanced; all stocks sold on January 1, 2009
- Portfolio rebalanced semiannually

Bull market: March 2003–September 2007: 92.2%, 81.4%
Bear market: October 2007–February 2009: –32.2%, –32.2%
Bull market: March 2009–April 2011: 16.3%, 63.1%
Bear market: May 2011–December 2011: 6.1%, –4.8%
Full period: March 2003–December 2013: 68.8%, 151.4%

Cumulative return (y-axis): –40, 0, 40, 80, 120, 160%

Notes: The initial allocation for both portfolios is 40% U.S. stocks, 16% international stocks, and 40% U.S. bonds. The rebalanced portfolio is returned to this allocation at the end of each June and December. Returns for the U.S. stock allocation are based on the Dow Jones U.S. Total Stock Market Index through April 2005 and on the MSCI US Broad Market Index thereafter. Returns for the international stock allocation are based on the MSCI All Country World Index ex USA, and returns for the bond allocation are based on the Barclays U.S. Aggregate Bond Index.

Source: Vanguard, using data provided by Thomson Reuters Datastream.

Note: We believe your strategic planning process should start with a thorough analysis of your current situation, including where you are financially right now; where you want to be; and whether you have enough resources to last throughout your retirement, and if not, what else you can do. It should factor in your income, assets, liabilities, family information, legal and tax accounting information, and insurances, as well as your overall goals and objectives.

Your written financial plan should also address your goals and objectives. It should include specific allocation and distribution strategies.

We can't stress enough the importance of maintaining and updating your plan. You should expect to receive a written overview of where you are at regular intervals. Your advisor should be able to help guide you and/or update your plan whenever you experience life changes. This will help you stay on track in meeting your goals.

## RULE 15. DEVELOP A PLAN WITH A LONG-TERM HORIZON IN MIND, BUT BE SURE TO MAKE ADJUSTMENTS ALONG THE WAY.

Diversification is key for a long-term portfolio. It's important to re-balance and re-focus your goals.

## *RULE 16. DON'T OUTLIVE YOUR MONEY.*

This is the biggest financial concern most retirees have. Our One-Page Analysis is a summary of where you are in meeting the goals you are working toward, as set forth in your financial plan. It provides accountability to clients who want to know where they are, where they should be, and what they need to do to get there. While some clients are comfortable spending down their retirement savings, the decision to do so should be an educated one.

# RUGGIE
## WEALTH MANAGEMENT

**Strength in Numbers**
Tavares | Winter Park
The Villages | Clermont
352.343.2700
Ruggiewealth.com

## WHAT'S YOUR NUMBER?

**Assets**

$1.4M

$1.3M  **\*$1.373M**

$1.2M

$1.1M

$1.0M

Client:  Joe & Mary Smith

### Annual Distribution Calculator

| GOAL | LAST 12 MONTHS |
|------|----------------|
| $69K | $29K |

### Family Index Number

Concerned  > 6%

Cautionary  5-6%

Great
2.11%  < 5%

Material Assumptions include average annual return of 6% and annual inflation rate of 3%. The projections of information generated by this Ruggie Wealth Management Financial Independence Roadmap regarding the likelihood of various investment outcomes are hypothetical in nature, do not reflect actual investment results, and are not guarantees of future results. The simulations are based on assumptions, and there can be no assurance the projected or simulated results will be achieved or sustained. This presents only a range of possible outcomes. Actual results will vary with each use and over time, and such results may be better or worse than the simulated scenarios. Clients should be aware that the potential for loss (or gain) may be greater than demonstrated in the simulation.

How do you know if you're spending too much in retirement? There is a fine line between living for today and saving for tomorrow. Your financial advisor should help you stay on the right side of it.

What should your advisor look at?

- Your assets and projected retirement income, including pensions and Social Security, along with your living expenses – mortgage, car payments, and travel – to determine whether you can comfortably cover your bills.

- Your timeframe for retiring – Delaying retirement by even a year or two can improve your future cash flow significantly. Not only does extra time in the workforce allow you to continue contributing to your individual retirement account (IRA) or 401(k) plan, but it also gives your nest egg the chance to deliver compounded returns longer.

- When you should start taking Social Security – This answer differs depending on the situation. Some should take it early, some should take it later, while others should apply and suspend.

- Your projected withdrawal rate – This is a key factor in whether your retirement savings will last as long as you do.

- Your emergency funds – Emergency funds do not have to be in cash or a cash equivalent. In fact, within our strategy, we recommend you have a conservative pool in your investment portfolio that covers 10 years of your income needs in retirement, rather than putting aside a cash equivalent of living expenses for a specified period (such as 6 months). Putting aside too much cash may mean you're not earning as much on your money as you could be.

- How the cost of care could impact your nest egg – A 2013 survey by Genworth Financial found at least 70% of people over 65 will need long-term-care services and support at some point in their lifetimes. The median annual rate for a private nursing-home room was $83,950 in 2013, up from $67,525 in 2008.

## RULE 17. IF YOU'RE NOT MEASURING IT, YOU AREN'T MANAGING IT.

We can't stress enough the importance of reporting and accountability. Your advisor should strive to eliminate as many layers of complexity in reporting as possible to give you the most understandable and convenient view of how your investments are performing and how you're doing meeting your financial goals.

# IV. Ask how your advisor is compensated

### *RULE 18. PAY FEES, NOT COMMISSIONS.*

How you pay someone to give you advice or manage your investments speaks volumes about whether the advice best serves the advisor or you. If product sales are mixed with advice, the potential for conflicts of interest increases, and objectivity may be compromised.

There are inherent concerns when an advisor is compensated solely by commissions. Of the many issues with a commission-based structure, the two biggest ethical dilemmas are:

1. Potential commissions earned by the advisor may drive their ultimate recommendation

2. If the advisor makes a lump-sum commission on your entire investment portfolio, what are the incentives for him/her to provide ongoing management for you?

A typical insurance product, such as an annuity, whether fixed, indexed, or variable, has an upfront commission to the advisor/agent typically in the 7% range, but I have seen some commissions as high as 15%. If the salesperson can make 7% of your money upfront by getting you to sign a few forms versus 1% annually in advisory fees for actually doing financial planning and managing your wealth (services which are naturally labor-intensive), ask yourself: Which compensation structure is that representative more likely to find advantageous to his or her bottom line?

The reality is that upfront commissions are recuperated by the insurance company through the use of various behind-the scenes schemes, such as increased hidden investment costs like that of index spreads, index cap rates, and internal fees found in annuity contracts (all of which decrease performance) and surrender fees, many of which start north of 15% during the first year. Surrender fees also decrease liquidity.

In my personal experience, dealing with prospects has shown me that commission-based salespeople are less likely to maintain ongoing contact with retirees if they have made their revenue upfront and there is no opportunity for additional sales in the immediate future. If they do reach out, it is often for another sales pitch.

### RULE 19. FEES SHOULD BE TRANSPARENT AND COMPETITIVE.

Your fees should align your advisor's interests with yours. When your portfolio does better, you should do better.

## RULE 20. YOUR ADVISOR SHOULD BE INVESTED IN A SIMILAR FASHION AS YOU.

Advisors should eat their own cookies. Ask if they take the same recommendations for their personal accounts that they recommend for yours.

# V. Who you gonna' call?

*RULE 21. IN AN IDEAL WORLD, AN ADVISOR KNOWS WHAT HE OR SHE IS DOING AND CARES ABOUT CLIENTS.*

Having been involved in coaching groups with many other financial advisors across the country, and based on my own personal experience, I've come up with a simple rule of thumb: I believe 10% of financial advisors really know what they are doing and really care about helping the people they counsel.

Another 10% don't know what they are doing and also don't care about helping their clients; these are the ones you really have to look out for, the "bad apples," as the saying goes.

Then there is the majority, who either don't know what they are doing, yet truly care about their clients, or have the knowledge base to have a good, positive impact on their clients but don't have the care or empathy to truly assist those clients.

**Note: Trust your intuition. Most people intuitively know whether the person they are going into a financial relationship with is a good fit. What happens to your money impacts YOUR quality of life, not that of your advisor.**

### RULE 22. ROBO-ADVISORS SHOULD NOT BE THE FINANCIAL ADVISORS OF THE FUTURE FOR MOST RETIREES.

Today, I cannot pick up a financial periodical without an article about robo-advisors. Robo-advisors are a class of automated investment programs that provide 'investment management' with minimal human intervention.

The simple reason robo-advisors are no threat to real advisors is that the services they offer are nothing like the comprehensive financial planning process offered by a true financial planner. The low-cost offering of robo-advisors generally begins and ends with setting an asset allocation. In other words, they're not actually financial advisors at all.

Robo-advisors will likely have a huge impact over the long-term on the financial industry, as they will appeal to newer generations as well as individuals looking for some form of assistance but at a lower price point.

However, when the chips are down, as they were in 2008, most people want an advisor they can speak with, who knows their situation; their dreams, goals, and aspirations; and with whom they can meet face-to-face. Many robo-advisors will dust off the old "set-it-and-forget-it" mentality. The problem is that set-it-and-forget-it doesn't take into account changing market and economic conditions, life changes, or any of the factors that can cause your plan to veer off course. A plan that encourages you to cross your fingers and hope something good will happen isn't really a plan at all.

### RULE 23. BE ABLE TO MEET THE ACTUAL PEOPLE MAKING YOUR INVESTMENT DECISIONS.

Whether in person, at in-person events, or during conference calls, you should have the opportunity to meet the person or people making decisions about your investments.

### RULE 24. DON'T RELY SOLELY ON JOURNALISTS AND TV PERSONALITIES FOR INVESTMENT ADVICE.

Need serious medical advice? You may watch *The Doctors* on television or get information from an online resource like WebMD. Both of these can be good tools; however, when it comes to your health, nothing replaces the advice of a trusted, knowledgeable physician or healthcare professional.

Think about it: Would LeBron James and Aaron Rodgers sharpen their skills just by reading a magazine? Would a company consider opening a facility in another state without speaking with an attorney?

We believe a healthy retirement requires choosing your financial advisor as carefully as you choose your heart surgeon.

A good advisor doesn't work for ratings. A good advisor doesn't have to be entertaining. And a good advisor talks to the specifics of your situation, not to the masses.

## RULE 25. THE MORE THINGS CHANGE, THE MORE THEY STAY THE SAME.

Today, investors face more complexity, technology, and options for investing than ever before. Still, even with the evolution in technology and the participation of new industries and markets, investing fundamentals remain largely unchanged. Keeping up with the newest strategies or techniques won't guarantee your success as an investor any more than not doing so will ensure failure. The goal is to make fewer mistakes and to make them less often than others.

# Playing by the rules

We all need rules to live by. Rules tend to make things fairer. Take the game of baseball, for example. Without rules, there would be no way to play the game or determine a winner. While baseball changes the rules from time to time to make the game more interesting, safer, or fairer, when you watch the game, you are comforted knowing that everyone has to play by the rules.

Ruggie Rules are valuable because they encourage order and make goals and expectations clearer.

We hope that by memorializing these rules, you will feel more empowered, secure, and confident to ask questions before making important decisions about your financial future.

# Why I dislike annuities

How you pay someone to give you advice or manage your investments speaks volumes about whether that advice best serves the advisor or you. If product sales are mixed with advice, the potential for conflicts of interest increases, and objectivity may be compromised.

Annuities have lots of bells and whistles that make them sound appealing to many investors, but when you truly evaluate these contracts, you find that most investors do not realize what they are giving up in the form of fees, lack of return, liquidity, or income design to get these benefits.

That's only the start of why I dislike annuities. Annuities are cost-prohibitive, not easily understood, and oversold, especially to retirees.

- They are cost-prohibitive because they generally carry larger internal costs, which reduce performance for the investor.

- Their promises of principal protection and guaranteed income streams sound alluring, but when you look under the hood, many of these products fall short of even modest expectations.

- Annuities are often misunderstood because they are fairly complex instruments. I've read hundreds of annuity brochures, prospectuses, and disclosure documents, none written in plain English. I've actually had annuity salespeople who sell significant amounts of annuities not be able to properly explain to me all the details within the annuities they sell to their clients. Scary, right?

- Many annuities are sold for their "guaranteed income benefits," which can increase regardless of market direction. That sounds good, right? The illustrations do a good job of showing the 'growth' to your future income, but what is often left out are the realities of these products' capabilities.

A few examples of how annuities become expensive are shown below; it isn't surprising for us to see annuities where most, if not all, of these apply.

- Participation/Index Rate: The actual percentage of the underlying index's return that an annuity holder earns. A participation rate of 50% means that you only get half of the index's return.

- Performance Cap: The maximum percentage of the index's return that you are credited. If the market is up 10% but you have a cap of 3%, then you can't earn more than the cap, regardless of the excess, which is kept by the insurance company.

- Market Value Adjustment (MVA): A monetary adjustment to the annuity's cash value that applies when you withdraw funds in excess of the "free amount." The MVA is a mechanism whereby the insurance company passes on its interest rate risk to contract holders. When rates rise, the MVA is negative; when rates fall, it is positive. In many contracts this MVA can apply even after surrender, so many people are stuck even after they've had their money tied up for years or decades.

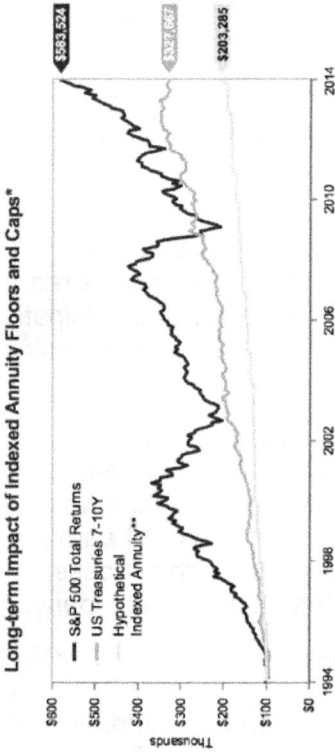

Long-term Impact of Indexed Annuity Floors and Caps*

S&P 500 Total Returns
US Treasuries 7-10Y
Hypothetical
Indexed Annuity**

$583,524

$387,063

$203,285

*Source: Global Financial Data showing returns from 12/31/1993-12/31/2013; as of 02/11/2014.
**Hypothetical annuity indexed to the S&P 500 with a 1% floor, 5% cap, 100% participation rate.

- Then there is the "guaranteed income or living benefit," the mother of all pie-in-the-sky arrangements. Here, the insurance company promises to increase your contract's future income capability at a certain rate each year; often the lingo used can give you the impression that you're 'earning' a certain rate, but in reality this is not real money that you could walk away with, but rather a level of funds from which you can draw on an annual basis at a specified distribution rate at a future point. This, too, is sometimes painted to be a rate of return; for example, "This annuity pays 7%." In today's low-interest-rate environment this isn't likely to be the same as if you had a CD that pays 7%. Both are unicorns, by the way. Rather than a rate of return, this is a distribution rate, meaning the rate at which you can receive payments from your account from its income benefit base.

- In theory, it sounds appealing for your income ability to increase over time and for you to be able to draw a guaranteed amount of funds. However, consider the fact that, when it comes time to distribute funds, the insurance company will first return to you *your own money* at a particular distribution rate and that, in reality, you'd have to live a very long time to (1) Get back your own money, (2) extract the full value of the "income base," and (3) recoup the costs you paid for that benefit. The good deal falls apart.

For example, if you're 70 years old with a contract worth $100,000 but an "income base" of $200,000 that will be paid out at 5% for life, you'd have to live 20 years to get that $200,000. Keep in mind that the first $100,000 is more or less your own money, so perhaps by the time you're 90 years old, your annuity is actually working the way it should in theory. That's not a good deal, regardless of the spin your advisor puts on it, and that doesn't even account for what your funds could have done for you had they been invested differently over the same period of time.

Perhaps the biggest fallacy in annuity sales is that you can have your cake and eat it too, which is to say, your annuity contract can give you market-like returns without market-like risk. Yes, some index contracts can allow you to participate in some of the upside of an index, such as the S&P 500, but how much of that index are you likely to earn?

As mentioned before, with caps, participation rates, and spreads, even during a bull market like the one we saw between 2009 and 2015, many of these contracts barely reached 2% annual returns. To a risk-averse investor that may sound appealing, but would that same investor buy a 7-, 10-, or 15-year 2% bond? Common sense says this isn't a reasonable rate of return for a period of time that long, yet this is the reality of some of these products.

That being said, in a few situations annuities could make sense, and there are "fee-based" annuities available, which lower the cost to the purchaser, thereby enhancing the ultimate return the client receives. However, because these don't offer big paychecks for annuity salespeople, they're hardly ever the products of choice, even when one would hypothetically make sense for a consumer.

# Ruggie Wealth

**Your health, wealth, and happiness in retirement are a function of many things.**

It's hard to imagine, but from now until 2030 Baby Boomers will reach age 65 at the staggering rate of 10,000 a day. Increased life expectancy has left many people unprepared for the cost of a healthy, enjoyable retirement – one that has the potential to last for decades.

Living a retirement full of activity, with decades of health, happiness, and prosperity, depends, to an ever-increasing degree, on the action you take today.

Ruggie WealthCare[sm] is a unique financial planning process that puts verbs in sentences and strategies into action.

Ruggie Rules advocate on behalf of investors. In the case of those nearing or entering retirement, they don't just address growing and preserving wealth, they aim to grow and preserve quality of life and peace-of-mind throughout your golden years.

By helping you control what you can (financially) and plan for what you cannot, we believe you will find that Ruggie Rules can help you live a better life.

Let us help you create your own unique Ruggie WealthCare[sm] Plan. Call 352.343.2700 for your free consultation. Experience the Ruggie Wealth difference.

# About the authors

**Thomas H. Ruggie, ChFC®, CFP®**
President

Tom has been in the financial services industry since 1991 and has appeared on CNBC, Fox News, PBS, and CNN Financial News. He has been quoted in a multitude of publications, including the *Wall Street Journal*, the *New York Times*, *InvestmentNews*, and *SmartMoney*.

- Barron's Top 1,200 Financial Advisors[1]; 50 Fastest-Growing RIA Firms[2];

- Top 100 Wealth Managers[3]; Top RIAs/List of Fastest-Growing Firms[4];

- Top 100 Independent Advisors[5]; Top 100, Top 40 Most Influential Advisors[6];

- Top Wealth Managers[7]; Top Wealth Advisors[8]

1. Barron's February 2015, February 2013, February 2009; 2. Financial Advisor Magazine 2011; 3. Advisor One 2011 4. Financial Advisor Magazine 2013, 2011, 2010; 5. Registered Rep Magazine 2011, 2010; 6. 401k Wire 2011, 2010; 7. Wealth Manager Web 2011, 2010; 8. Worth Magazine 2006, 2007, 2008

**Louis Shinaman, ChFC®, CEP®**
Senior Wealth Advisor

- Chartered Financial Consultant, Registered Options Principal, Certified Estate Planner

- Financial services industry since 1996

- Has traveled overseas as a renowned public speaker, focusing on investments and technical analysis

- Fluent in Spanish

**Jorge A. Romero, CFP®**
Senior Wealth Advisor

CERTIFIED FINANCIAL PLANNER™ practitioner
(CFP®)

- Financial services industry since 2004

- Served honorably in the United States Marine Corps

- Has a B.A. in Political Science and Pre-Law, along with a Minor in Latin American Studies from the University of Central Florida

- Fluent in Spanish

# Eight questions to ask before choosing your advisor...or changing to a new one

|  | Yes | No |
|---|---|---|

1.    Is your portfolio created according to your specific needs, taking into account your investment objectives, time horizon for the assets, cash flow needs and other factors specific to you?

2.    Do you get <u>proactive</u> service from your own Investment Advisor, who will keep you up-to-date on your portfolio?

3.    Do you have the opportunity to meet the actual people making investment decisions, in-person meetings, at in-person events, or conference calls?

4.    Has your Advisor earned professional designations such as a Chartered Financial Planner® or CERTIFIED FINANCIAL PLANNER professional? Received professional recognition by leaders in the field such as Barron's®? Provided insights on a national basis to media outlets?

5.    Do you get a disciplined approach to your investment strategy that goes beyond picking stocks?

6.    Does your advisor offer a wide range of investment styles and products? Can he or she adjust strategy based on a forward-looking view of market conditions?

7.    Is your advisor a Registered Investment Advisor who works in YOUR best interest?

8.    Are your advisor's fees transparent and competitive? Do they align your advisor's interests with yours? When your portfolio does better, do you do better?